Grandma's
HOUSE

LaKisha L Minnis

WestBow Press books may be ordered through booksellers or by contacting:

WestBow Press
A Division of Thomas Nelson & Zondervan
1663 Liberty Drive
Bloomington, IN 47403
www.westbowpress.com
844.714.3454

ISBN: 978-1-6642-0580-2 (sc)
ISBN: 978-1-6642-0598-7 (e)

Library of Congress Control Number: 2020918178

Print information available on the last page.

WestBow Press rev. date: 9/29/2020

WESTBOW
PRESS®
A DIVISION OF THOMAS NELSON
& ZONDERVAN

In Loving Memory of Estella Minnis

Grandma's House

The bell ring, it's 3:15. "Gather your belonging students, and let's head outside for dismissal." Said Mrs. Harman. I am so ready to go outside under the tree and see my grannie, said LaKisha.

Jeremiah, Zachary, Corry, Emia, Luetisha, and LaKisha all ran under the tree to greet their grandmother. "Hello Madea!" said the children in unison. Hey! How was your day at school? Good! The children replied.

We walked over the hill and through
the field to grandma's house.

Go on in the house children and wash your hands for a late lunch. We cannot wait to eat; I know that you prepared a bunch. "Yes I did!" said Madea.

Great northern beans, mashed potatoes, meatloaf, and peach cobbler. Oh! Don't forget your glass of water.

Then comes a knock at the door. "Someone is at the door!" yelled Zachary. "Who is it!" shouts Madea. "It's us!" little voice we hear!

In comes Aunt Bobbie and her crew. "Leave the door open" says Aunt Bobbie, here comes Mary Lou! In comes Louise and the Duke boys with a lot of laughter and cheering noise.

Out of the room comes Rubystein, "not so loud everyone! I can't hear a thing."

Later comes in, Mildred, Vickie, Jerry, Boddie, and Jermaine. "Well... I am glad that everyone has finally made it," says Madea.

As we all gather around the table to bless the dinner; we all reflect on what a blessing it is to have a "Madea", and a great dinner at Grandma' House.

The End

Printed in the United States
By Bookmasters